DESIGNING WITH GRAPHIC ARTS

DIY Visual Projects

Ruthie Van Oosbree

Abdo & Daughters
MIDDLE GRADE NONFICTION
An imprint of Abdo Publishing
abdobooks.com

ABDOBOOKS.COM

Published by Abdo Publishing, a division of ABDO, PO Box 398166, Minneapolis, Minnesota 55439. Copyright © 2023 by Abdo Consulting Group, Inc. International copyrights reserved in all countries. No part of this book may be reproduced in any form without written permission from the publisher. Abdo & Daughters™ is a trademark and logo of Abdo Publishing.

Printed in the United States of America, North Mankato, Minnesota
102022
012023

THIS BOOK CONTAINS RECYCLED MATERIALS

Design: Emily O'Malley, Mighty Media, Inc.
Production: Mighty Media, Inc.
Editor: Liz Salzmann
Projects: Tamara JM Peterson
Cover Photographs: Mighty Media, Inc. (front insets and poster), Nastya Sokolova/Shutterstock (back cover), Photographee.eu/Shutterstock (front background)
Interior Photographs: Glenn Pierce/Flickr, p. 59 (right bottom); guitarfish/Flickr, p. 24 (bottom); iStockphoto, pp. 4, 5 (both), 6 (top left), 12 (paintbrushes, paper, red ink, brayer, stencil, paper cutter), 13 (all), 14, (top), 15 (left bottom, right top, right bottom), 16 (right), 18, 22 (top, right top, right bottom), 23 (top right), 24 (middle), 25, 44 (left middle), 45 (middle left), 54, 57, 60 (top), 61 (bottom); Ivan Sutherland/Wikimedia Commons, p. 9 (left bottom); JR P/Flickr, p. 58; Katsushika Hokusai/Wikimedia Commons, p. 11 (bottom); Loz Pycock/Wikimedia Commons, p. 10 (bottom); Mighty Media, Inc., pp. 26 (paper), 28, 29, 30 (printed pillow), 32, 33, 34 (poster), 36 (step photos), 37 (step photos), 38, 40, 41, 46, 47, 48, 49, 50, 51, 52, 53; NYCB/Wikimedia Commons, p. 59 (right top); Shutterstock Images, pp. 3, 6 (top right and bottom), 7, 8 (top), 9 (right), 11 (top), 12 (stamps), 14 (left middle, left bottom, right), 15 (left top, left middle), 16 (left), 17, 19, 20, 21 (both), 22 (left), 23 (top left, bottom left, bottom right), 24 (top), 26 (background), 30 (background), 34 (background), 36 (band photos), 37 (band photos), 42, 44 (left top, left bottom, right top, right middle), 45 (top, middle right, bottom), 55 (both), 56, 59 (top), 60 (bottom), 61 (top); StacieBee/Flickr, p. 10 (top); Thomas Hawk/Flickr, p. 59 (left); Wikimedia Commons, pp. 8 (bottom), 9 (left top)
Design Elements: Mighty Media, Inc., Shutterstock

Library of Congress Control Number: 2021970090

PUBLISHER'S CATALOGING-IN-PUBLICATION DATA

Names: Van Oosbree, Ruthie, author.
Title: Designing with graphic arts: DIY visual projects / by Ruthie Van Oosbree
Other title: DIY visual projects
Description: Minneapolis, Minnesota : Abdo Publishing, 2023 | Series: Craft to career | Includes online resources and index.
Identifiers: ISBN 9781532198861 (lib. bdg.) | ISBN 9781098272791 (ebook)
Subjects: LCSH: Graphic arts--Technique--Juvenile literature. | Visual communication in art--Juvenile literature. | Crafts (Handicrafts)--Juvenile literature. | Do-it-yourself products industry--Juvenile literature.
Classification: DDC 760--dc23

CONTENTS

Making Crafts a Career 5

The Basics 7
Getting Started 19
Make This! 27
Beyond the Projects 43
Careers In Graphic Arts 57

Glossary 62
Online Resources 63
Index 64

MAKING CRAFTS A CAREER

What's your passion? Think about that hobby or activity that challenges, excites, and fulfills you—the one that makes you lose track of time. Maybe it's drawing, painting, sewing, or woodworking. Or perhaps there's something you've always wanted to try, such as graphic design or metalworking.

Craftspeople make life more interesting. Their creations delight viewers while often serving a practical purpose. A well-crafted table is both useful and beautiful. A well-designed concert poster can draw fans in while providing important information. The details of a jacket or hat reflect an individual's personality and style.

Arts and crafts have been enriching the lives of artists and audiences for thousands of years. Many craftspeople have found ways to use their passion to support themselves financially, turning their craft into a career.

Anyone can become an artist. All you need is some basic knowledge, a little creativity, and a lot of patience. This book is full of tips, tricks, and techniques to get you started on the road from craft to career. What will you make?

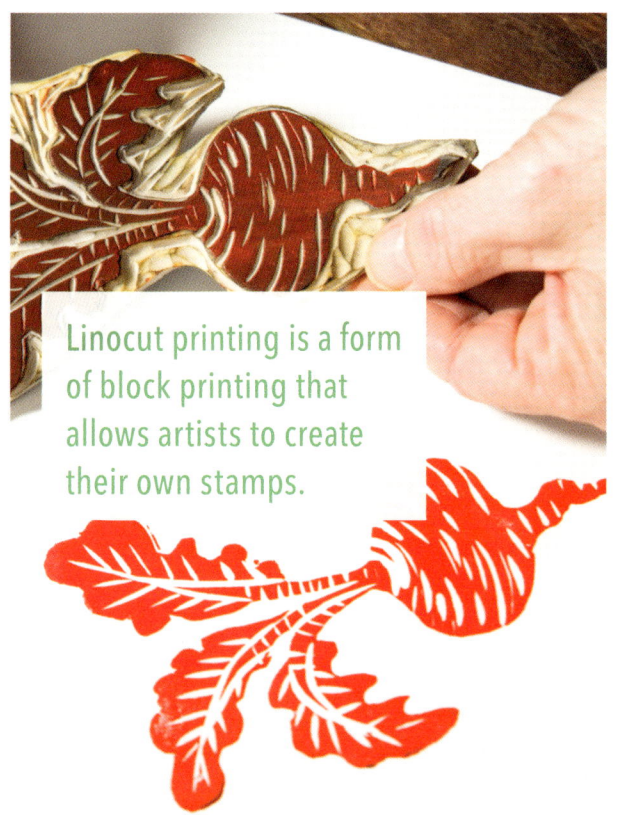

Linocut printing is a form of block printing that allows artists to create their own stamps.

Digital graphic design is a form of graphic arts and a popular career field.

Line and tone are important aspects of most graphic art forms.

THE BASICS

WHAT ARE GRAPHIC ARTS?

The term *graphic arts* can refer to many different forms of visual art. It covers most art forms done on a flat surface. These include painting, printmaking, drawing, photography, calligraphy, and more. Computer-designed pieces are also works of graphic art.

Though it encompasses many different art forms, *graphic arts* usually refers more specifically to works that rely more on line and tone rather than color. These can include drawings, engravings, and especially printed works.

Graphic artists can make prints in many different ways. Techniques range from simply using stamps and ink to using special equipment to screen print. Some forms, such as woodblock and linocut printing, require artists to carve designs into the surface of wood or other material. The carved designs are then inked and pressed onto paper or another surface. Heat or chemicals can also be used to create designs that can be inked and printed.

Graphic arts may get confused with graphic design. Graphic design is a form of graphic arts. It uses design concepts to communicate particular messages or information. Graphic designers arrange text and illustrations together to do this. Graphic design also often refers to computer-created art. There are forms of graphic design that are done by hand. But people tend to think of digital processes when they think of graphic design.

Graphic arts in general aren't necessarily intended to convey information. Artists may create works of graphic art just for beauty. Or they may craft something practical.

Letterpress stamps are used to typeset text for print.

HISTORY OF GRAPHIC ARTS

Graphic art is one of the oldest art forms. Its history can be traced back to cave paintings from 45,000 years ago. Writing developed in the Middle East around 3000 BCE. At first, people wrote on slabs of clay. Later, people wrote on rolls of papyrus and animal skins.

Paper was developed in China in 105 CE. By 600, the Chinese were using woodblock printing. Art could be shared by making many prints of the same design.

Movable type was developed by Chinese artist Bi Sheng in the 1040s. This involves arranging wooden or clay blocks carved with letters and symbols. The blocks are held together and inked for printing on paper. This allowed people to print many copies of the same text.

Around 1450, German printer Johannes Gutenberg invented a new type of printing press. This machine used metal instead of wood blocks for letters. This new printing press could print more copies of texts more quickly and for a lower cost.

During the Industrial Revolution, lithography and photography were invented. These art forms made art more affordable. People didn't have to be rich to buy art. In the 1900s, the computer introduced a whole new way to create graphic art. Today, different forms of graphic arts are used for a variety of purposes.

GRAPHIC ARTS TIMELINE

45,000 YEARS AGO
People in many places around the world create cave paintings.

ABOUT 3000 BCE
Early forms of writing develop.

600 CE
Woodblock printing is used in China.

1040s
Bi Sheng develops movable type in China.

1450

Johannes Gutenberg invents a new printing press that is cheaper and more efficient.

1796
Lithography is invented in Germany.

1826
French inventor Nicéphore Niépce takes the first successful photograph.

1880s
Ottmar Mergenthaler invents the linotype, a typesetting machine.

1963
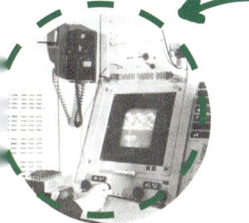

Sketchpad, the first software that could be used to create an image on a computer, is introduced.

1985
Microsoft Paint enables people to create images on their home computers.

1990
Photo editing computer program Adobe Photoshop is released.

American pop artist Andy Warhol used screen printing in many of his pieces, including his iconic prints of actor and model Marilyn Monroe.

Printmaking has often been used to work for political change. In the 1960s and 1970s, printmaker Emory Douglas created prints for the newspaper of the Black Panther Party for Self-Defense.

GRAPHIC ARTS & CULTURE

Graphic arts have had a major impact on human cultures. Printing, and especially the printing press, allowed people to share art and information more widely. As a result, more people learned to read and had access to knowledge.

Examples of graphic art from throughout history help us learn about the past. But graphic arts aren't just objects in museums. They are also part of everyday culture. People wear T-shirts with screen-printed graphics. Newspapers and websites include photographs. Computer-designed graphics are used in ads, websites, and posters. Artists use graphic techniques to create beautiful and meaningful art.

The meanings of different graphic arts elements, such as colors and symbols, vary across countries and cultures. Red may be negative in Western cultures. But in some Eastern cultures, red has positive associations. And people of different religious backgrounds may use colors associated with their faith.

Graphic arts trends and styles also vary across cultures. Some cultures may use more crowded, compact designs, while others may favor cleaner, more minimalist designs. Color palettes, fonts, illustration styles, and use of white space are a few other elements of graphic arts that may differ between cultures.

Ukiyo-e is a Japanese style of woodblock art. Nature and history are common subjects. *The Great Wave off Kanagawa* by Katsushika Hokusai is an example of *ukiyo-e*.

TOOLS OF THE TRADE

Here are some of the tools you will need as you dive into the world of graphic arts!

BASIC ITEMS

PAPER

Paper is a necessary part of many graphic arts projects. Paper comes in a variety of colors, glosses, textures, and thicknesses.

INK

Printmaking requires ink. You may just use a simple ink pad, or you may need ink specially made for block printing, screen printing, etching, or another technique.

BRAYER

A brayer is a small roller that helps distribute ink evenly on a stamp or other printing surface.

STAMPS

Most craft stores carry a wide variety of premade stamps in many different designs and sizes.

STENCILS

Stencils have the outline of designs cut into them. Ink, paint, or a different substance is spread over the stencil, coating only the cutout areas.

PAPER CUTTER

A paper cutter has its own ruler so that you can line your paper up and cut it in straight, exact lines.

STANDARD ART SUPPLIES

Graphic arts include paintings and drawings. Grab paint and paintbrushes, markers, pencils, and any other art supplies you like using.

TABLET OR COMPUTER

As you begin experimenting with computer-designed graphics, you'll need a tablet or computer. You can also use it to research projects and find helpful instructional videos.

GLUE

You might glue magazine cutouts to a poster to make a collage, or you might cut shapes out of paper or other materials to glue onto a card. Basic school glue will work in many cases, but you may need special glues if you're gluing fabric or other materials besides paper.

PRINTER

A printer will allow you to print out designs you create on your computer. You can also print stencils, photos, and other elements. If you don't have a printer at home, see if you can use one at your school or public library.

SPECIALTY TOOLS

The tools below will help you take your graphic arts projects to the next level!

SCREEN-PRINTING KIT

In screen printing, ink is pushed through a stencil on a mesh screen and onto a surface such as fabric or paper. Screen-printing kits include the mesh as well as a squeegee, ink, and other supplies.

SCREEN-PRINTING TRANSPARENCIES

Rather than using a premade stencil, you can use transparencies and photo emulsion on the screen. The design is printed on the transparency in black and the rest of the sheet is clear. This allows photo emulsion to react with UV light and harden in the area surrounding the design.

FABRIC FOR PRINTING

You may wish to print designs on fabric items, such as T-shirts, tote bags, or pillowcases. You could also print on plain fabric that can then be used for another project.

STAMP-ARRANGING TOOL

Some tools allow you to arrange stamps into a design and press them together onto paper. These may be called stamp or letterpress platforms or stamping presses.

EMBOSSING, CUTTING & LETTERPRESS MACHINES

These are more advanced machines for working with and printing on paper and other materials.

CARVING BLOCKS

Designing your own stamps is a fun way to customize your projects. Blocks are available in a range of materials, from erasers to linoleum. There are also some specialty products designed to be easy to carve.

CARVING TOOLS

Carving tools are necessary for carving your own stamps. They may be sold as one handle with a range of blades. Or you may be able to purchase a set of carving tools with different blades.

CALLIGRAPHY SUPPLIES

There are a few types of calligraphy tools. These include markers, dip pens, and fountain pens. They have different nibs for different types of calligraphy. You can also use a calligraphy brush. They come in a variety of thicknesses and materials.

DESIGN SOFTWARE

Design software provides ways to learn new techniques. Computers at your school or public library may have design software you can use. There are also free programs you can download or use online. Always check with a parent, teacher, or librarian for help determining whether online software is safe to use.

MATERIALS MATTER

Paper is used in many graphic arts projects. But there are many different types of paper. Follow this guide to choose the right paper for your project.

	What It Is	Why It Matters
Thickness	Paper comes in a wide range of thicknesses. Often a paper's thickness is measured by its weight. In the United States, this is usually the weight in pounds of 500 sheets of the paper.	Thin paper bends, folds, and can be cut or torn more easily than thicker paper. Certain inks may bleed through thinner papers. Thinner paper may cost less than thicker paper.
Texture	Some papers are made with textures you can see and feel. Certain papers, such as handmade paper, may be naturally more textured than standard printing paper.	Textures can be attractive. But they may cost more and present challenges in writing and printing.
Coating	Some papers have a thin coating to make them smooth.	The coating creates a sort of seal on the paper. Some coatings may be more expensive.

Considerations for Different Uses

- Thick paper is good for making greeting cards, business cards, and posters. If you're using an ink or paint that bleeds easily, choose thick paper.
- Thin paper is good for tracing.
- Medium-weight paper is good for flyers, books, brochures, and light inks that are less likely to bleed.

- Certain types of printmaking, including lithography and screen printing, will work better on smoother papers.
- Stamping and calligraphy can be done on textured paper, but it will be more challenging.

- Uncoated papers are best for projects with a lot of text, as glare from coated paper can interfere with reading.
- Uncoated papers work best for printmaking, bookmaking, embossing, and folding.
- Coated papers work well for computer-designed graphics and other types of high-detail images.

GETTING STARTED

SETTING UP YOUR SHOP

Many craftspeople find they do their best work when the have a dedicated workspace. There, the materials they need are within arm's reach and they can let their creativity shine. Where will you set up your workshop?

A graphic arts studio can be as big as a room or as small as a kitchen table. No matter where you decide to work, here are a few things to keep in mind:

- You will want a large, clean, flat surface for laying out paper, fabric, and other supplies.
- There are many tools available for graphic arts. Choose quality but affordable basic tools to begin with.
- Graphic arts projects can take time. Make sure you have a safe, dry place to store your works in progress until you can work on them again.
- If you'll be using any machines or a computer, you'll need a sturdy table near an outlet.
- Wear a protective mask and work in a well-ventilated space when using chemicals or any toxic materials. For projects that use ink or paint, wear an apron to help protect your clothes.

MAKER TIP

Many graphic arts projects use some kind of ink. Keep your ink in good condition with careful storage. Follow the manufacturer's storage instructions. Ink should be kept in closed containers. It should not be allowed to get too hot or too cold. Extreme temperatures can affect the thickness of the ink.

BE SMART WITH YOUR ART

Your shop is set up and you're ready to make! There are a few things to keep in mind as you begin your exploration of graphic arts.

CHOOSE YOUR TOOLS WISELY. The right tools can make or break a project. Make sure all your tools are ready for crafting. Check that power cords are not frayed and that all tools are clean, sharp, and in proper working order.

SAFETY FIRST. Graphic arts projects often require chemicals and sharp tools. You are in charge of staying safe in your shop! Work carefully and slowly at all times, especially when using sharp tools. Check for any warnings on ink containers and other packaging. Read the instructions or get a lesson on using any tools or materials unfamiliar to you.

TAKE YOUR TIME. Graphic arts projects take patience! Plan your project before beginning. Gather all the materials you need and research any new techniques you will be using. Consider where you'll set down wet ink rollers, squeegees, and ink tubes or jars as you work. Prepare materials carefully. Then work slowly, especially early in a project when you are still mastering techniques.

PRACTICE, PRACTICE, PRACTICE! It's a good idea to try new techniques on scrap materials. That way, you can work out any problems that may come up, and you'll be that much more prepared when you work on more expensive materials.

BE FLEXIBLE. Projects often don't go exactly as planned. That's part of the fun! Don't be afraid to change a material, technique, or even the original plan to solve a problem that comes up during your project. Your brain is your most important tool!

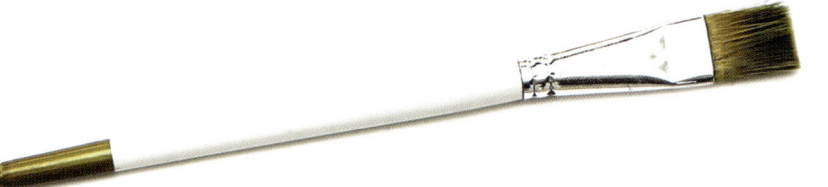

TIPS & TECHNIQUES

The more graphic arts projects you do, the more you'll learn what materials and methods you like best. Here are a few tips and techniques to get you started.

EXPERIMENT WITH MATERIALS

Many graphic arts projects can be done with a variety of materials. Try using papers of different textures and thicknesses. See what types of ink, paint, pens, or markers you prefer. Make stamps out of different materials to see what's easiest to carve and what creates the best final product.

stamp. Start with a small amount of ink. You can always add more!

STAY STAIN-FREE

Whenever you are going to use ink, cover your work surface with newspapers or an old tablecloth. Protect the floor underneath your workspace with newspaper or drop cloths.

USE SUPPLIES WISELY

Many beginning printmakers make the mistake of using too much ink. This can lead to blotchy prints from ink filling the carved-out areas of a

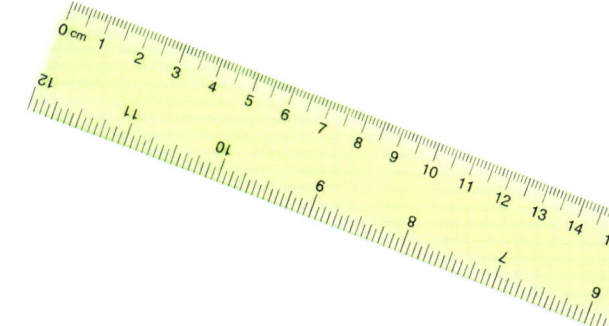

START WITH A SKETCH

Whether you're carving a design into a block or designing a poster on your computer, draw your vision on paper first. When you're satisfied with your sketch, you can refer to it as you work on the project itself.

CARVE IN REVERSE

Remember that stamps will print a mirror image of what is carved into them. This is especially important to keep in mind if you're carving letters or numbers. Carve them backwards. If you need a guide, hold a correctly drawn letter up to the mirror and carve that mirrored image in your block. Also, keep in mind that the part you carve out of the block is what won't show up on the print. You need to carve around the design that you want to stamp.

MEASURE & WORK SLOWLY

Some mistakes in graphic arts projects may mean having to start over. There are some ways to avoid that frustration! As you work, have patience. Work slowly to avoid mistakes. Take time to measure and then double-check your measurements before cutting something. Do test prints on scrap materials. Complete project steps in order. But don't worry if you have to start over occasionally. It's an unavoidable part of many crafts.

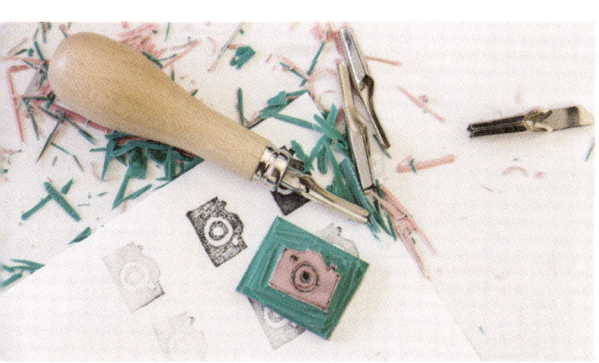

GRAPHIC ARTS 101

Here is some basic information about different areas of graphic arts.

PRINTMAKING

Printmaking is the general term for creating art using ink on paper or other flat surfaces. There are four types of printmaking:

- Relief printing: carving into a block around the design. The design sticks out so ink can be rolled onto it. This is also called block printing.
- Intaglio: carving a design into a surface rather than cutting around the design. Ink is rolled over the surface, and then the surface is wiped clean. The ink stays in the carved design. Then paper is pressed onto it for printing.
- Stenciling: using stencils to print designs.
- Lithography: drawing designs onto a surface with a greasy material and treating it with chemicals and water so ink only sticks to the design.

Linocut is a simple form of relief printing that uses linoleum blocks or sheets. A helpful way to do it is to copy the design onto the block to form a guide for carving. This can be done with tracing paper and transfer paper.

- First, draw the design on plain paper.
- Lay tracing paper over the design and trace it.
- Lay carbon paper or another transfer paper on the linoleum block. Lay the tracing paper with the design facedown on the carbon paper. Tape them to the block.

- Trace over the design again. The transfer paper will leave the design behind on the block. Then you can begin carving!

> When you're comfortable with cutting linoleum, you may wish to experiment with other relief printing methods, such as woodblock printing, or to experiment with intaglio or lithography. You'll need help from someone trained in these methods to get started.

BOOK BINDING

Making books is a form of graphic art. This includes the binding process. There are many ways to bind books. Some popular methods include:

> Perfect binding: gluing edges of pages together and covering the edge with card stock.
> Sewn binding: sewing pages together with thread or string.
> Comb and spiral binding: joining pages by punching holes in them and threading a coil through the holes.
> Saddle stitch binding: using either small stitches or staples along the center fold of the book to hold the pages and cover together.

DIGITAL GRAPHIC DESIGN

Graphic design software can be expensive. But there are many websites that allow people to do graphic design for free. These sites provide templates and elements such as shapes, decorative text, illustrations, and other graphics. Some have photos you can use.

You can find templates for commercial purposes, such as logos, ads, and business cards. You'll also find templates for invitations, social media posts, résumés, and more. Some sites give you the tools to design video elements and animations! Popular websites that allow free downloads include Canva, Stencil, and Adobe Creative Cloud Express.

MAKE THIS!

HANDMADE PAPER

You can buy many different kinds of paper. But making your own paper gives your graphic arts project a unique touch. The materials are easy to find—you can reuse scrap paper that would otherwise be recycled. Plus, making paper is creative! Once you've mastered basic papermaking, you can experiment with different types of paper and adding fun materials.

STUFF YOU NEED

- paper (several kinds or one kind)
- paper shredder (optional)
- large bowl or plastic container
- water
- blender
- plastic bin (larger than the papermaking screen)
- papermaking screen
- clean rag
- drying board (board or cardboard covered with an old bedsheet)
- fan
- rolling pin
- blotting paper
- heavy books

1

2

> **TIP**
> You can add personality to your paper by mixing in different materials. Try adding glitter, dried pressed flowers, grasses, or food coloring.

1 Tear the paper into very small pieces, or use a paper shredder.

2 Put the paper in a large bowl or plastic container. Cover the paper with water. Let it soak for at least two hours.

3 Put the paper and water mixture in a blender. Blend it until it is smooth paper pulp.

4 Fill a large, flat bin with 3 inches (7.6 cm) of water. Mix three handfuls of pulp into the water.

5 Slide the papermaking screen into the bin from one side, then quickly push it evenly to the bottom. Move it back and forth a few times, then gently lift it out of the water.

6 Let the water drip into the bin for a few minutes. Wipe any excess pulp off the frame with a clean rag.

5

7

7 Hold the screen above the drying board. Then quickly flip the screen over. Set the pulp side against the board. It may take a couple tries to get a feel for this technique. Remove the screen by lifting one corner and slowly peeling it away.

8 Repeat steps 1 through 7 to make more sheets of paper.

9 Let the paper sit with a fan blowing on it until it is almost dry. Then use a rolling pin to smooth the paper.

10 Stack the paper with blotting paper between each sheet. Flatten the stack under heavy books until the paper is dry.

**What else can you do with paper?
Find out how to make it your way on page 46!**

SCREEN-PRINTED PILLOWCASE

Take your first steps into the world of printing with a screen-printing project. Turn a plain pillowcase into an interesting piece of bedding by screen printing a design onto it. You'll end up with a cool, eye-catching pillow—and sweet dreams!

STUFF YOU NEED

- photo emulsion kit
- screens with frame
- transparency sheets for printer, or black marker and clear plastic sheets
- clear tape
- sink with running water
- old soft toothbrush
- masking tape
- pillowcase
- board that is slightly smaller than the screens
- fabric ink
- squeegee

2

3

> **TIP**
> Change up the colors of your design! You can print the design in any color or combination of colors you choose.

1 Go into a dark room. Mix the emulsion and apply it to the screens. Follow the instructions that came with the emulsion kit.

2 Prepare the transparencies. You can print your design on transparency film or draw it on clear plastic using a black marker. If your design has more than one color, put each part that will be a different color on its own transparency.

3 Put a transparency on each screen. Use clear tape to hold the transparencies flat. Place them under a bright light for 30 to 60 minutes. Follow the instructions that came with the emulsion kit.

4 Carefully lift the transparencies off the screens. Rinse the screens. Use an old, soft toothbrush to remove any emulsion that didn't harden. Let the screens dry.

5 The areas not covered by emulsion are where the design will be. Check the screens for any areas not covered by

6

7

emulsion that are not part of your design. Place masking tape on the underside of the screen to cover these areas.

6 Lay the pillowcase flat on a board and tape it in place with masking tape.

7 Place the first screen on the pillowcase. Cover the screen with one color of fabric ink. Use the squeegee to press the ink through the screen onto the pillowcase. Carefully remove the screen.

8 If you are using multiple colors, repeat step 7 with the other screens. Be sure to let each color dry completely before applying the next one.

> **What else can you print?**
> **Find out how to make it your way on page 48!**

GARAGE-BAND POSTER

Spread the word about your favorite band with a handmade poster! Use collage, hand lettering, photography, painting, and more to create different effects and add a personal touch. You can apply the techniques you learn from this project to make movie posters, a school project, or your own artwork.

STUFF YOU NEED

- band photos
- computer and printer
- posterboard or large sheet of paper
- markers
- scissors
- glue
- paint, paintbrush, colored paper, colored tape, washi tape, stickers (optional)

1

2

1 Find one or more cool photos of your band and print them out as large as you can. The photos should not be bigger than your posterboard.

2 Decide what information you want to have on your poster. You can use markers to write the text on the posterboard or type it on a computer and print it out.

3

4

3 Glue the photos and text to the posterboard.

4 Trim the pieces that stick out past the sides of the posterboard, unless you want them to stick out.

5 Jazz up your poster with paint, colored paper or tape, washi tape, or stickers!

What other handmade graphic arts projects can you create? Find out how to make it your way on page 50!

COMPANY LOGO

Commercial design, or design used to sell products or services, often uses computer-designed graphic art. Get started in commercial design by designing an attractive and unique logo for your own company. You'll need your artistic talent, but you'll also need to think about the business side of design for this fun project!

STUFF YOU NEED

- paper
- pencil
- markers
- scanner or camera
- computer and printer
- graphic design program such as InDesign or Canva

1

2

TIP

If you're struggling to come up with logo ideas or to decide on a layout, check out any templates in the design program or look at other company logos for inspiration.

1 To create your own company logo, you'll first need a company! Think of an idea for your business and come up with a name. Find or design an image for your logo. Write down and sketch out your ideas.

2 Once you are satisfied with your sketched image, draw the artwork in marker on a clean sheet of paper.

3 Scan the artwork into your computer or take a photo of it and upload it.

4 Import the image into a graphic design program.

5

6

5 Type the company name. Try using different fonts until you find one that fits the image you want your company to have and who your clients will be. Also make sure it's easy to read.

6 Test out different color combinations, still considering who your clients will be. Try to figure out what colors they would like.

7 Try different sizes of text and arrange the text and artwork different ways.

8 Save your final logos and use them on all of your company's materials.

What other business materials can you create? Find out how to make it your way on **page 52**!

BEYOND THE PROJECTS

MAKE IT YOUR WAY!

Following instructions to complete a specific project is a great way to learn and master new techniques. But now it's time to let your creativity shine. Design and create your own projects by mixing and matching the different techniques you learned in this book! Keep these tips in mind as you're planning and executing your project.

GET INSPIRED

Inspiration is all around you! The internet is full of tutorials, videos, and images that can give you project ideas and teach you new techniques. Nature is full of colors and patterns just waiting to be used in a graphic arts project. Explore the graphic art form traditions in your own and other cultures. And look at what graphic arts are popular on different products at stores you like. Then, think of ways you can make your mark on these projects.

USE WHAT YOU HAVE

Sometimes, materials you already have on hand can direct the project you will create. Do you have a plain T-shirt or tote bag you don't use much? Screen print a design on it to give it some personality. Erasers? Create small stamps. Old magazines? Make a collage.

PROBLEM-SOLVE

Plans change! Materials run out! Techniques fail! Don't sweat your mistakes. Instead, look at them as opportunities to learn and grow. Sometimes, an unexpected issue might send your project in a new direction you never would have thought of. Be open and flexible, and you'll create a project that is completely unique and entirely you.

COLLABORATE

Stuck? Don't be afraid to ask for help! A classmate might bring a new perspective to your project. A teacher or parent might know just how to solve the problem you're having. You can also seek expert advice from graphic arts organizations in your area or online.

THE ELEMENTS OF DESIGN

Anytime you're planning a new graphic arts project, consider the elements of design. These are the basic units of a visual image. There are many ways to approach these elements when imagining and creating.

FORM

This is the space a piece of art occupies. Graphic arts are usually two-dimensional. But they may cover three-dimensional objects.

LINE

A line is the connection between two points. Lines can be horizontal, vertical, diagonal, straight or curved.

SHAPE

Shape is the outline of a certain object or area. A shape can be geometric, organic, or abstract.

SPACE
Positive space is the area that the subject of the art takes up. Negative space is the empty space around the subject. In graphic arts, negative space is sometimes referred to as white space. Artists use space to draw viewers' eyes to certain areas.

TEXTURE
This is the way an object feels or appears to feel. It can be soft, rough, smooth, fuzzy, and much more!

COLOR
Color is often used to convey the mood of a piece of art. Many designers use a color wheel to choose a color scheme for their work.

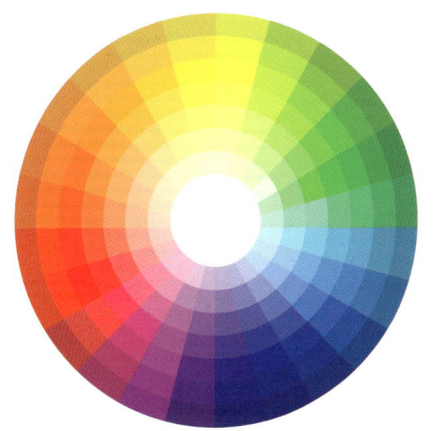

GREETING CARDS & MORE

After you've made some sheets of your own paper, have some fun figuring out all the different ways you could put the paper to good use!

Create your own "staple" for binding with a piece of wire you carefully cut and bend.

A gift given in a handmade box is like giving two gifts in one!

Try sewing the pages of a card together.

BLOCK PRINTING & MORE

You can print patterns and shapes with almost anything—leaves or bark from a tree, decorative buttons, and more. Once you find or make a design you like, use it to print many copies of the same thing!

Try swapping out the color of the shirt or the color of the ink for fun variations.

Use items from nature as stamps to make cool abstract designs.

WALL ART & MORE

Try a variety of graphic art forms with handmade art, from painting to mixed-media wall art. Even the way you bind a book can be art! There are no rules when it comes to creating your own artwork.

Write your own book. Illustrate it with drawings or photographs. Then, have fun figuring out how to put all the pieces together.

Try mixing many materials you like to make a fun wall hanging. Paper, wood, and metal are just some of the things you can add to your piece.

Bold stripes and blocks of paint can be arranged in any formation. And throwing a paint-filled water balloon at an empty canvas can be a fun way to create your work of art!

BROCHURES & MORE

When you start a company, using a computer to design your materials can help your company look more professional. You'll also be able to print as many items as you need. Remember that computers help you produce your designs, but it all starts in your imagination. How do you envision your company's commercial designs?

Don't forget to consider your target audience and the colors and images they'll be drawn to.

Think about where you can advertise so your target audience will see your designs and information.

Make business cards to give to clients so they can find you again, and recommend you to their friends.

What Next?

Your graphic arts project is a wrap. Now what? Don't pack away your supplies just yet! It's time to finish and style your hard work.

FINISHING TOUCHES

Examine your finished piece. If you made prints, look through them and choose the one that you think came out the best. Do you want to add any adornments, such as gluing on decorative paper? Think about how you want to use what you made. Will you use it yourself, give it as a gift, or display it somewhere for people to admire? Will you photograph it to share on social media or maybe even sell it?

DISPLAYING PROJECTS

There are tons of way to use and display graphic arts projects. You can distribute flyers and mail greeting cards. You can wear printed T-shirts and carry printed tote bags. You can prop books and cards on a shelf. And you can share graphic design creations on social media or use them to design a blog.

PHOTO STYLING TIPS

Follow these simple tips and tricks to make your projects pop!

> - Choose a space that is well lit. Portable ring lights can be a great way to set up a photo studio wherever you are.
> - Arrange your project with items that relate to the work's look or function. But make sure the items don't overshadow the art!
> - Choose a background that makes your project stand out.
> - If you made a wearable item, such as a printed T-shirt, have friends and family model your creation or model it yourself.

CAREERS IN GRAPHIC ARTS

BECOMING A GRAPHIC ARTIST

There are many paths to turning your love of graphic arts into a career. You might become a photographer, illustrator, or printmaker. These careers all have fine arts paths, where you create art meant to be appreciated for its beauty and meaning. They also have paths for commercial work or freelance work.

Graphic design is a popular field that lets you put your design and technology skills to use. There are many different paths within graphic design, including marketing and ad design, web design, publishing design, and more.

Graphic artists may get college degrees in fields such as drawing or printmaking. People interested in computer-designed graphics may specialize in graphic design. They learn the artistic, design, and technical skills they will need for a career in graphic arts.

But not every graphic artist gets a formal education. Some might learn the skills they need through apprenticeships or on-the-job training. Many other artists are self-taught. They may eventually turn a favorite arts hobby into a business by selling their creations online or in shops.

NJIDEKA AKUNYILI CROSBY

Njideka Akunyili Crosby is a Nigerian-born artist who works in Los Angeles, California. She creates mixed-media pieces that combine collage, painting, drawing, and printmaking. Her art also combines African and American art influences and traditions.

GRAPHIC ARTISTS AT WORK

Meet some artists who are moving and shaking in the graphic arts world!

SHEPARD FAIREY

Shepard Fairey is an American graphic artist known for screen-printed designs. He combines illustration, typography, and digital graphic design in his art. Much of his work is related to his political activism. One of his most popular prints is a poster of Barack Obama with the word *Hope* beneath his portrait. This print was adopted by the 2008 Obama presidential campaign. Fairey continues to make prints and murals with activist messages.

DERRICK ADAMS

Derrick Adams is a mixed-media artist and professor of fine arts in New York City. He uses painting and collage, and he also makes sculptures, videos, and performance art. Adams' award-winning work explores Black life, culture, and identity in the United States.

LAUREN HOM

Lauren Hom is an American graphic designer and illustrator known for her hand-lettering work. She does freelance design work and helps companies and people with their branding. She also offers lettering courses. She published a book based on her blog *Daily Dishonesty*. Her work has won many typography and communications awards.

Intaglio artists etch designs into metal plates, roll ink over the entire plate, then wipe off all the ink except what's inside the etched design.

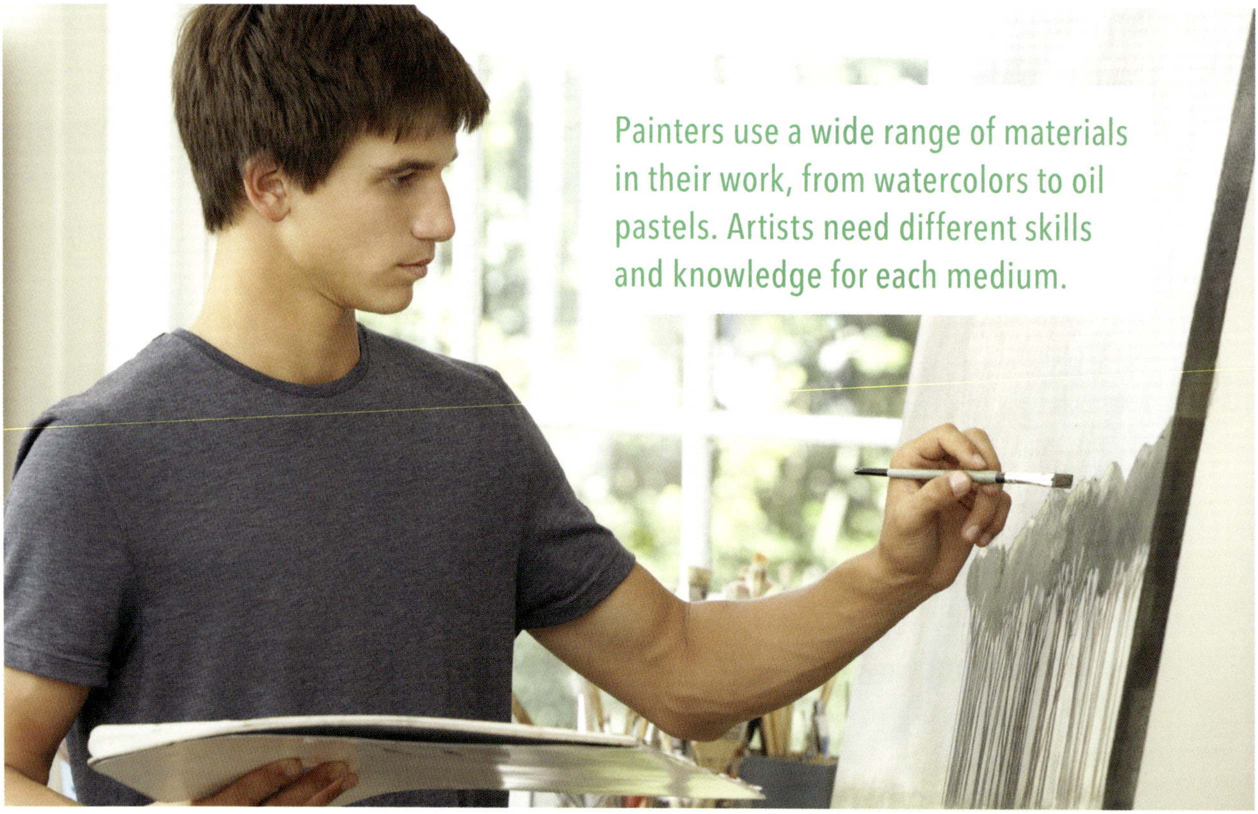

Painters use a wide range of materials in their work, from watercolors to oil pastels. Artists need different skills and knowledge for each medium.

DO WHAT YOU LOVE!

Your project may be complete and your studio cleaned up, but your graphic arts journey is far from over! Think about the projects you made. How do they reflect your identity as an artist? What did you learn from them? What would you do differently next time? What new techniques would you like to experiment with?

This book explored many graphic art forms, including paper making, screen printing, block printing, and graphic design. But there are even more graphic arts to discover. You can design prints using intaglio techniques or different materials. You can explore illustration styles such as those in comic books and cartoons, and learn about animation. You can learn about photography and photo editing or different painting techniques. You might find courses teaching advanced skills in your favorite graphic art form or a new type of graphic art you're not familiar with.

Creating graphic art is a fun and fulfilling hobby, but where else could your love of this craft take you? Maybe one day you'll design a website, start your own Etsy shop, or become a famous printmaker. So gather your supplies, ink your stamps, and get to work. Your imagination is the limit!

Cartooning is a type of graphic art. Cartoonists draw comic strips, comic books, and more. Some use their skills in animation.

GLOSSARY

apprenticeship—an arrangement in which a person learns a trade or craft from a skilled worker.

audience—a group of readers, listeners, or spectators.

calligraphy—handwriting or lettering that is decorative or artistic and usually created with a special pen or brush.

collage—art composed of a variety of materials, such as paper and cloth, glued onto a surface.

concert—a musical performance or show.

emboss—to decorate with a raised pattern or design.

etch—to make a pattern or design on a hard surface with a substance that eats into the surface, such as acid.

intaglio—a printmaking technique where a design is carved into a surface such as a metal plate, the plate is inked, and the ink is wiped from the surface, leaving ink only in the carved design. Paper or another material is then pressed into the carved design for printing.

linoleum—a floor covering made of linseed oil, gums, ground cork, sawdust, and pigment on a canvas or burlap backing.

lithography—a printmaking technique where a design is drawn on stone or a metal plate with a greasy material. The surface is then treated with water and chemicals so the ink only sticks to the design.

nib—the tip of a pen.

papyrus—a paperlike material made from the papyrus plant and used by ancient people to write on.

perspective—a particular attitude toward or way of looking at something.

photo emulsion—a material that hardens when exposed to light. Short for photographic emulsion.

printmaking—using a prepared surface, such as a block or plate, to transfer an image from that surface to another material.

relief printing—printing done using a block or other material that has been carved so the design is on the surface and everything that isn't printed has been carved below the surface.

scheme—an organized design.

technique—a method or style in which something is done.

template—in graphic design, a preset computer file created with a general layout or design for a specific purpose and that can be customized.

tutorial—a lesson on how to do something. Tutorials are often presented through media such as videos or computer programs.

typography—the art of arranging and styling text for printing or graphic design.

ventilated—exposed to fresh, freely moving air.

ONLINE RESOURCES

To learn more about graphic arts, please visit **abdobooklinks.com** or scan this QR code. These links are routinely monitored and updated to provide the most current information available.

INDEX

Adams, Derrick, 59
Adobe Creative Cloud Express, 25
animation, 25, 61

Bi Sheng, 8
block printing, 8, 12, 15, 23, 24, 25, 48–49, 61
blotting paper, 27, 29
book binding, 25, 46, 50
bookmaking, 17, 25, 50

calligraphy, 7, 15, 17
Canva, 25, 39
careers, 5, 57
carving, 7, 8, 15, 22, 23, 24
carving tools, 15
collage, 13, 35–37, 43, 58, 59
comb and spiral binding, 25
computer, 7, 8, 11, 13, 15, 17, 19, 23, 35, 36, 39, 40, 52, 57
Crosby, Njideka Akunyili, 58
cutting machine, 15

design software, 15, 25
displaying projects, 55
drawing, 5, 7, 13, 23, 24, 32, 40, 50, 57, 58

education, 57, 61
elements of design, 44–45
embossing, 15, 17
embossing machine, 15
engraving, 7
erasers, 15, 43
etching, 12
Etsy, 61

fabric, 5, 11, 13, 14, 19, 31, 33, 43, 48, 55
Fairey, Shepard, 59
folding, 16, 17, 25
fonts, 11, 41

glue, 13, 25, 35, 37, 55
graphic design, 5, 7, 25, 39, 40, 55, 57, 59, 61
Gutenberg, Johannes, 8

history, 8, 11
Hom, Lauren, 59

illustration, 7, 11, 25, 50, 57, 59, 61
Industrial Revolution, 8
ink, 7, 8, 12, 14, 16, 17, 19, 21, 22, 24, 31, 33, 48, 61
ink roller, 21
intaglio, 24, 25, 61

letterpress, 14, 15
letterpress machine, 15
linocut printing, 7, 24
linoleum, 15, 24–25
lithography, 8, 17, 24, 25

metalworking, 5
movable type, 8

Obama, Barack, 59

painting, 5, 7, 8, 12, 13, 17, 19, 22, 35, 37, 50, 51, 58, 59, 61
paper, 7, 8, 11, 12, 13, 14, 15, 16–17, 19, 22, 23, 24, 27–29, 35, 37, 39, 40, 46–47, 51, 55, 61
  coating, 12, 16–17
  texture, 12, 16–17, 22
  thickness, 12, 16–17, 22
paper cutter, 12
papermaking screen, 27, 28–29
performance art, 59
photo emulsion, 14, 31, 32–33
photography, 7, 8, 11, 13, 14, 25, 31, 35, 36–37, 40, 50, 55, 57, 61

printing press, 8, 11
printmaking, 7, 12, 17, 22, 24, 57, 58, 61
projects
  block printing, 48–49
  brochures, 52–53
  company logo, 39–41
  garage-band poster, 35–37
  greeting cards, 46–47
  handmade paper, 27–29
  screen-printed pillowcase, 31–33
  wall art, 50–51

relief printing. See block printing

saddle stitch binding, 25
safety, 15, 19, 21
screen printing, 7, 11, 12, 14, 17, 31–33, 43, 59, 61
  kit, 14
  transparencies, 14, 31, 32
selling, 39, 55, 57
sewing, 5, 25, 47
squeegee, 14, 21, 31, 33
stamp-arranging tool, 14
stamping, 7, 12, 14, 15, 17, 22, 23, 43, 49, 61
stenciling, 12, 13, 14, 24, 25
storage, 19
styling, 55

tablet, 13
typography, 59

video, 13, 25, 43, 59

woodblock, 7, 8
woodworking, 5
workshop, 19, 21, 22